ECOSYSTEMS OF THE WORLD

TUNDRA ECOSYSTEMS

by Tammy Gagne

Content Consultant
Robert Hollister, PhD
Associate Professor
Grand Valley State University

Core Library

An Imprint of Abdo Publishing
abdopublishing.com

abdopublishing.com

Published by Abdo Publishing, a division of ABDO, PO Box 398166, Minneapolis, Minnesota 55439. Copyright © 2016 by Abdo Consulting Group, Inc. International copyrights reserved in all countries. No part of this book may be reproduced in any form without written permission from the publisher. Core Library™ is a trademark and logo of Abdo Publishing.

Printed in the United States of America, North Mankato, Minnesota
032015
092015

Cover Photo: Incredible Arctic/Shutterstock Images
Interior Photos: Incredible Arctic/Shutterstock Images, 1; John Pitcher/iStockphoto, 4; Shutterstock Images, 7, 9 (background), 9 (bottom left), 9 (middle top), 25, 30, 36, 43; Sergey Uryadnikov/Shutterstock Images, 9 (bottom right); Dan Bach Kristensen/ Shutterstock Images, 9 (middle left); Jim H. Walling/Shutterstock Images, 9 (top); iStockphoto, 9 (middle bottom), 10, 12, 27, 34; iStock/Thinkstock, 15; Jennifer Stone/ Shutterstock Images, 16, 45; Gregory A. Pozhvanov/Shutterstock Images, 19; Nadezhda Bolotina/Shutterstock Images, 20, 28; Delmas Lehman/Shutterstock Images, 22; Steve Bower/Shutterstock Images, 32; Gary Braasch/Corbis, 39; Sergey Timofeev/ iStockphoto, 40

Editor: Arnold Ringstad
Series Designer: Becky Daum

Library of Congress Control Number: 2015931041

Cataloging-in-Publication Data
Gagne, Tammy.
 Tundra ecosystems / Tammy Gagne.
  p. cm. -- (Ecosystems of the world)
Includes bibliographical references and index.
ISBN 978-1-62403-857-0
1. Tundra ecology--Juvenile literature. 2. Tundra--Juvenile literature.
I. Title.
577.5--dc23
                                                             2015931041

CONTENTS

CHAPTER ONE

LIFE IN THE TUNDRA

A tiny arctic fox raises its pointy ears. It hears a polar bear in the distance. The fox begins moving toward the sound.

The long cold winter on the tundra is finally coming to an end. It will still be a while before the plants start growing again, though. Food has been scarce for the arctic fox lately. Most of the birds flew south long ago.

Arctic foxes live in the northernmost areas of Asia and North America.

The fox relies on polar bears for most of its meals. Once a bear finishes eating, the fox eats the scraps. Even a polar bear usually cannot eat a whole seal.

With its white fur, the fox easily blends in with the snowy terrain. Just in case the bear is still nearby, the fox moves slowly and quietly. It does not want to become the bear's next meal.

A Cold, Harsh Place

Life on the arctic tundra can be harsh. This frosty ecosystem is found in the northernmost areas of the globe. Alaska, Canada, Greenland, and Russia all have vast tundra regions. As the weather gets colder each year, many animals leave the tundra. They return in the spring. The animals that stay have special traits to help them survive the frigid winter.

Limited Wildlife

The tundra is home to many types of plants and animals. However, the variety is not as great as in other parts of the world. This lower biodiversity is due in part to a harsh climate. Only those species that have adapted to the cold can survive.

Polar bears are the largest carnivores of the tundra.

The Alpine Tundra

The Arctic is not the only place where tundra is found. Tundra also exists in high elevations throughout the world. These ecosystems are known as alpine tundra. As in the Arctic, only specially adapted plants can grow in alpine tundra. However, there are no trees. The alpine tundra is sometimes called "the land above the trees" for this reason.

Polar bears and arctic foxes have dense winter coats. Seals and walruses have a heavy layer of insulating body fat called blubber.

Everything that lives in the tundra plays a role in the ecosystem. Animals eat other animals and plants. Even moss plays an important part. It helps keep the soil moist. This allows plants to grow in the summer. Each living thing depends on other organisms for its survival.

A Tundra Food Web

The food web of the arctic tundra includes both large and small wildlife. Polar bears eat smaller animals, such as seals. Foxes scavenge on leftover seals. Both foxes and owls hunt rabbits. The rabbits survive on plants, such as mosses that grow on rocks. The sun provides energy for the moss to grow. How does this food web help you understand how animals survive in the tundra?

CHAPTER TWO

THE AIR UP THERE

The tundra is the world's coldest ecosystem. The temperature usually falls between 10 and 20 degrees Fahrenheit (-12 and -6°C). A layer of frozen soil called permafrost plays a key role in the ecosystem. It can extend up to 5,000 feet (1,524 m) below the ground. The cold air keeps the ground frozen for most of the year.

Even when the sun shines brightly, the tundra remains very cold.

Pools of water can form when permafrost thaws.

As summer approaches, the upper soils begin thawing. Ice and snow turn into shallow bogs and ponds. With the water's help, life flourishes in the tundra. Plants grow again. Insects pollinate flowers. They lay eggs in the wetlands. Birds return to the landscape. They feast on insects and lay eggs of their own.

Long Days, Short Season

The air in the arctic tundra becomes warm enough for a short growing season. The sun shines 24 hours a day for up to 60 days during the summer. This happens because of Earth's tilt. The northern hemisphere is tilted toward the sun in summer and away from the sun in winter.

The unique climate makes it possible for only certain kinds of life to survive in the tundra. Summer in the tundra is short, but it is warm and wet enough for some species to thrive.

Dry and Windy

Most of the year, the tundra is as dry as the

Alpine Permafrost

More than 20 percent of Earth's land surface has permafrost beneath it. Most of this soil has been frozen for thousands of years. Permafrost exists in both arctic and alpine tundra ecosystems. The closer an ecosystem is to the equator, the higher the elevation of the permafrost. In the northern United States, alpine permafrost is found at elevations of at least 8,000 feet (2,438 m). Far to the south in Arizona, however, it can only exist above 11,500 feet (3,505 m).

world's deserts. Very little rain or snow falls. Most tundra ecosystems only get between 6 and 10 inches (15 and 25 cm) of precipitation each year. However, the frozen soils trap this water. Sometimes it pools in shallow lakes. As a result of the damp soil, many parts of the tundra are considered both wetlands and deserts.

Winds on the tundra can blow at up to 60 miles per hour (97 km/h). This causes powerful windchill effects. The wind can make the temperature feel much colder than it is.

Standing Water

In most places of the world, rainwater drains into the soil. In the tundra, the permafrost leaves the rain with nowhere to go. Melting snow simply turns to standing water in this ecosystem. It then freezes and thaws with the changing seasons.

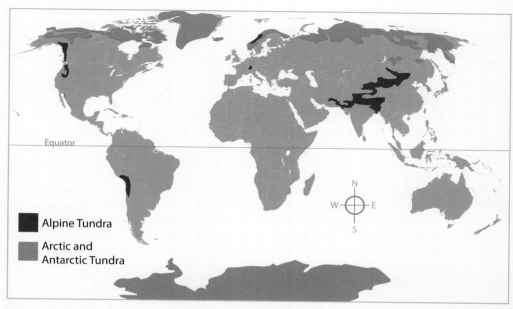

Where Tundras Are Found

Tundra ecosystems are found in many parts of the world. Arctic tundra is located in the far north. Alpine tundra can be found anywhere on the globe, as long as the elevation is high enough. The closer a mountain region is to the equator, the higher it must extend to include a tundra ecosystem. With that in mind, what can you tell about the tundra regions in South America and South Asia?

HARDY PLANTS AND LICHENS

Compared with many other ecosystems, such as rain forests, biodiversity in the tundra is low. Only specially adapted vegetation can grow in this cold environment. Still, more than 1,700 plant species manage to survive in the tundra.

Most of these plants are small. It is warmest near the ground. In the winter, the snow protects

Plants on the tundra grow low to the ground.

these small plants. Plants that grow too tall may be damaged or killed by winter winds.

Tall Plants

A key feature of the tundra is that it is nearly treeless. However, some of its taller plants blur the line between tall shrubs and short trees. They are often in areas where they are protected from the wind. The Alaska willow is one of the tallest plants found in the arctic tundra. It is able to grow only 20 feet (6 m) tall. The species is sometimes called a shrub rather than a tree. The Alaska willow is an important food source for moose.

The arctic willow is much smaller, at just

Special Features

Very few types of trees can grow in the tundra. In order to survive in this ecosystem, trees must have shallow root systems. They often grow outward, rather than upward. Tundra trees also need to be able to tolerate high winds and low temperatures. Most trees do not have these features, so the ones that remain are usually the strongest varieties. The result is low diversity.

The dwarf birch is adapted to live in the cold tundra climate.

7 inches (18 cm) tall. This tiny species is especially good at protecting itself. During the growing season, the arctic willow produces poison. The natural substance keeps insects from eating the plant's leaves.

The dwarf birch grows in thick bunches and has tough leaves. The harsh winds of the tundra help the species survive. When the wind blows, it spreads the dwarf birch's seeds to new areas.

Lichens provide food for the grazing animals of the tundra.

Moss and Lichens

Most plant life in the tundra consists of moss and lichens. Mosses are small plants that grow in dense clumps. Lichens sometimes look like mosses. However, they are made up of fungi and algae rather than plants. In the tundra, these organisms cover much of the ground. They are even found on rocks. One of the most common species is reindeer lichen, also known as caribou moss. It is named for the animals that eat it.

Reindeer lichen is grayish green. It is well adapted to the dry climate of the tundra. When sunlight and water are in short supply, this plant goes dormant. During this time it stops growing but does not die. When the sun and moisture return, reindeer lichen begins growing again.

FURTHER EVIDENCE

Chapter Three includes information about the plants of the tundra. What are some of the main points in this chapter? How does the environment of the tundra affect what kinds of plants grow there? Take a look at the website below. Does the information on the website support what you read in the chapter? Does it add any new evidence?

Surviving in the Tundra
mycorelibrary.com/tundra-ecosystems

CHAPTER FOUR

ANIMALS OF THE TUNDRA

Animals living in the tundra fall into two categories. The first are species that can survive there throughout the year. They are highly adapted to the extreme conditions. These animals find ways to keep warm despite the freezing temperatures and high winds. They also manage to raise their offspring during short periods of mild weather.

Tundra swans and other birds migrate for the winter.

Living Off the Land

Tundra swans split their time between the arctic tundra and warmer locations. They are known to travel up to 3,725 miles (6,000 km) each winter. When spring returns, so do the swans. Laying their eggs in the wetlands, the swans depend on plant life for both food and shelter. This species eats many types of underwater plants and insects. They reach below the surface with their long necks. They make nests from sticks. The swans line their nests with mosses and grasses.

The second group of tundra animals lives there only during the warmer times of the year. When the temperatures drop, these animals travel to more temperate regions. Most of the tundra's birds belong to this category. They fly to warmer areas for the winter.

Year-Round Residents

The tundra's top predator is the polar bear. This large hunter travels wherever food is available. Polar bears can swim great distances, even in icy waters. They have been seen as far as 200 miles (322 km) from land. The bears catch rides on floating sheets of sea ice.

Polar bears grab seals when the seals swim near the ice.

Polar bears are well suited to the tundra ecosystem. They have the heaviest coats of all bears. They also have blubber beneath their skin. This layer of fat serves two purposes. First, it keeps the bears warm. Second, it helps them float. Polar bears also have webbed feet, which aid with swimming.

Polar bears hunt seals, including ringed seals and bearded seals. Once the bears finish eating, other

Small But Numerous

When the snow melts and forms small pools across the tundra, the insect population explodes. Millions of blackflies, deer flies, and mosquitoes emerge from the expanding wetlands. Even arctic bumblebees and butterflies can be seen during the summer. Most of these insects will die before the coldest weather returns. Many become food for birds. Others simply cannot survive the freezing temperatures. Before they die, the insects lay eggs. The eggs can survive the tundra's brutal winter.

animals eat the leftovers. One of these animals is the arctic fox.

Like the polar bear, the arctic fox is well suited to the tundra. Its short ears and muzzle help it stay warm. The small surface area of these body parts means they lose less heat. The fox's thick coat and long furry tail also keep the animal warm. Even the soles of its feet are covered with fur.

Fair-Weather Residents

As winter comes to an end, many animal species return to the tundra. Birds are among the most common of these migratory animals. Ducks, geese,

Geese live near Iceland's lakes.

and loons are just a few of the many birds that move back to the tundra each spring. Caribou also migrate between the tundra and warmer regions.

Each plant and animal living in the tundra plays a role in the ecosystem. Most species serve as food for at least one other species. Arctic hares and caribou

Caribou move in huge herds.

eat the plants and grasses of this region. Hawks eat
the hares. Wolves feast on the caribou. Birds eat many
types of fish and insects. In this way, the animals of
the tundra depend heavily on one another.

Journalist Stanley Johnson watched the migration of the caribou from the tundra firsthand:

> We had been on the water a couple of hours already when Richard, scanning the shore with his binoculars, saw a lone bull caribou. The animal seemed to be heading towards a pinnacle of land which jutted out into the lake. We drove around in our boats to the other side of the promontory, then walked back along the shoreline to be rewarded, minutes later, by a close-up view of the young bull, maybe three or four years old, with an already magnificent spread or 'rack' of antlers on its head. This was the icing on the cake. I had a long-distance lens on my camera. I pointed it in the right direction. That young bull caribou raised its head, less than 50 yards away, sniffed the wind, and looked right at us, before breaking into a run and disappearing from view.
>
> Source: Johnson, Stanley. "Deer Diary." The Sunday Telegraph (London), September 28, 2014.

What's the Big Idea?

Take a closer look at this passage. How does Johnson feel about having the opportunity to witness the caribou migration? What can you tell about the caribou's attitude toward people based on its behavior?

CHAPTER FIVE

PEOPLE NEAR AND FAR

People have lived in or near the arctic tundra for thousands of years. Life in this region of the world is not easy. Often the nearest store is many miles away. Even in places with stores, the brutal conditions make it difficult to ship goods. Everyday items can be extremely expensive.

Many people living in the tundra exist largely off the land. They hunt to put food on their tables. They

The Inuit people have lived in Northern Canada for many generations.

Building roads through the tundra may harm ecosystems.

use plants for both food and medicine. With such a short mild season, they have learned to preserve plants and fish by drying them.

Respect for the Ecosystem

People who visit the tundra must be careful not to harm it. As harsh as it may seem, this ecosystem is delicate. Plants and lichens can be destroyed easily. All-terrain vehicles can trample them. Even hiking boots can cause damage. A single footprint can last for years in this fragile environment.

When outsiders visit the tundra, they are asked to be respectful of the ecosystem. Simply watching your step helps keep plants alive. Visitors should not remove anything from the tundra. With so few species, each one is vital to the survival of the others.

Bigger Dangers

Everything within the tundra ecosystem is connected. However, even people outside these regions can affect the tundra. Air pollution is a growing concern. Winds bring toxic chemicals, such as mercury, into the Arctic. Factories and other industrial buildings around the world release greenhouse gases into the atmosphere. These gases, which include carbon dioxide and methane,

Porcupine Caribou

Herds of porcupine caribou migrate through the tundra to Alaska each year. The caribou come to an area known as the Arctic National Wildlife Refuge each spring. The US government has set aside this area to protect animals. Many female porcupine caribou give birth to calves there. Drilling for resources in the Arctic could disrupt this process.

Air pollution can harm the tundra in several ways.

trap heat inside the atmosphere. The result has been rising temperatures around the world. This process is known as climate change. Warmer temperatures make it harder for many arctic species to survive.

Some companies are entering the Arctic for its resources. Large amounts of gas and oil lie below the ground. But harvesting these resources could devastate the tundra ecosystem. Events such as oil spills can harm tundra species.

Scientist Matt Wallenstein studies how changes in the environment are affecting the arctic tundra. In a blog post, he writes about the changes he has seen:

> *The climate is changing rapidly in the Arctic. Warming is occurring twice as fast here as in the rest of the world. And the results are visible from space. The short growing season is getting longer, and the plants are getting bigger and greener. What you can't see from space is that the microbes and other critters that live beneath the surface are waking up too. This "biotic awakening" sounds like a good thing, and it probably is if you are a microbe, but could be bad for us. That's because these microbes could open this carbon lockbox, releasing some of that banked soil carbon back to the atmosphere as carbon dioxide and methane. Because both of these are greenhouse gasses, that could further accelerate climate warming.*
>
> *Source: Matt Wallenstein. "Live from the Thawing Arctic Tundra: The Challenge of Communicating Complex Science to the Public." EcoPress. Colorado State University, June 6, 2014. Web. December 31, 2014.*

Back It Up

The author of this blog post is using evidence to support his point. Write a sentence describing his point. Then write down two pieces of evidence he uses to make the point.

TOMORROW'S TUNDRA

The future of the tundra is uncertain. Even the smallest changes in this environment can have lasting effects. Some organisms may even go extinct. Climate change is among the biggest threats to life on the tundra.

Temperatures in the Arctic have been rising for decades. The warmer air has led to an earlier onset of spring in the tundra. While this may not seem like a

Climate change may bring more melting to the permafrost of the tundra.

A Good or a Bad Thing?

With the arctic ice melting, polar bears come ashore earlier in the season. The available food sources are different this time of the year. The bears, which normally hunt seals, eat snow geese and their eggs instead. In recent years populations of this bird species have exploded in the Arctic. This plentiful food source could be good news for the polar bear, which has been declining in numbers. It could also cause some problems, however. Many geese are moving to other areas to avoid their new predators. These changes could have big effects on the future of tundra ecosystems.

problem, it has triggered many changes. Snow and soils melt earlier than usual, and plants begin growing sooner. Migratory animals return to the tundra several days earlier than they did just a few decades ago. What will happen if the temperatures keep rising?

The animals and plants of the tundra are adapted to survive the specific conditions of the tundra. When temperatures rise and seasons shift, organisms may suffer. For example, the timing of migrations

Scientists in the tundra study the ecosystem's plants, animals, and climate.

is closely tied to the availability of food. If these schedules change, animals may not have enough food to survive.

Solving the Problem

Scientists predict overall temperatures in the Arctic will continue to rise. The tundra ecosystems may see the sharpest rises. If nothing is done, the tundras of Alaska and Canada will warm up and turn to forests.

People are working to save the beautiful landscapes of the tundra.

The best defense the tundra ecosystem has is education. As people learn about the harm caused by climate change, they can make better choices. Simple steps, such as limiting electricity use and planting trees, can help. Electricity production is responsible for emitting greenhouse gases. Trees take in carbon dioxide, helping to reduce the amount of the gas in the atmosphere. Ordinary citizens can also urge their elected officials to take action.

Some climate change has already happened, and it will continue into the future. But people can work to slow its progress. The problem cannot be solved overnight. But if more people take it seriously, more of the unique plants and animals of the tundra can be saved.

EXPLORE ONLINE

Chapters Five and Six describe how climate change is impacting tundra ecosystems. The article below discusses scientific discoveries about these processes. As you know, every source is different. Compare the information in these chapters with the information in the article. Is any information the same in both sources? How do the two sources present information differently?

Climate and the Arctic
mycorelibrary.com/tundra-ecosystems

Arctic Tundra

Located in the northern hemisphere just below the North Pole, the arctic tundra is the largest tundra ecosystem in the world. It is home to about 1,700 different plant species and 48 mammal species, including caribou, polar bears, and wolves.

The Andes

Located in western South America, the Andes are one of the world's largest mountain ranges. The chinchilla, which is a popular house pet in the United States, lives in the alpine tundra of this region. The animal's soft, dense fur keeps it warm even in the coldest temperatures.

Rocky Mountain National Park

One of the best-known alpine tundra ecosystems is located in the continental United States. Rocky Mountain National Park in Colorado includes some of the highest mountain peaks in the country. The animals in the park range from the tiny deer mouse to the mighty elk.

Ukkusiksalik National Park

Canada's Ukkusiksalik National Park covers nearly 13,000 square miles (20,880 sq km). The protected area includes the Central Tundra Natural Region. This tundra ecosystem is home to numerous types of wildlife. Grizzly bears, muskoxen, and peregrine falcons are just a few of them. Although indigenous peoples, known as the Inuit, are allowed to hunt in the park, no humans permanently live in the region.

Yaks feed on tundra grasses.

The Himalayas

The Himalayas are found in South Asia. This alpine tundra ecosystem is home to the yak. Weighing between 1,000 and 1,200 pounds (454 and 544 kg), the yak is an immense creature. Despite its size, the yak moves about its mountainous home remarkably easily.

STOP AND THINK

Surprise Me

Chapter Six discusses how small changes in parts of the world outside the tundra are having a big impact on this ecosystem. After reading this book, what two or three facts did you find most surprising? Write a few sentences about each fact. Why did you find them surprising?

Another View

This book discusses how using natural resources in tundra ecosystems may harm the environment. As you know, every source is different. Ask a librarian or another adult to help you find another source about drilling for oil in the Arctic. Write a short essay comparing and contrasting the new source's point of view with that of this book's author. What is the point of view of each author? How are they similar and why? How are they different and why?

Why Do I Care?

Few people live in tundra ecosystems. Why should you care if the temperatures in these regions are rising? Who will be affected if the tundra disappears? Based on what you have read, write a paragraph describing the effects of these changes.

You Are There

This book discusses how wildlife in the tundra works together. Imagine you are living near the arctic tundra. How might you depend on the plants and animals in the region for your survival? How would your everyday life be different than your life now?

GLOSSARY

biodiversity
the variety of plants and animals living in a specific environment

blubber
a layer of body fat that keeps animals warm

dormant
alive but temporarily not growing

extinct
no longer existing

migratory
moving from one region or climate to another, usually on a regular schedule for feeding or breeding

permafrost
permanently frozen ground

pinnacle
a high, pointed peak

pollinate
spread reproductive material between plants, allowing the plants to reproduce

precipitation
water that falls to the ground as hail, mist, rain, sleet, or snow

promontory
a high point of land sticking out into the sea

LEARN MORE

Books

Benoit, Peter. *Tundra*. New York: Scholastic, 2011.

Rosing, Norbert, and Elizabeth Carney. *Face to Face with Polar Bears*. Washington, DC: National Geographic, 2007.

Taylor, Barbara. *Arctic and Antarctic*. New York: DK Publishing, 2012.

Websites

To learn more about Ecosystems of the World, visit **booklinks.abdopublishing.com**. These links are routinely monitored and updated to provide the most current information available.

Visit **mycorelibrary.com** for free additional tools for teachers and students

INDEX

ABOUT THE AUTHOR

Tammy Gagne has written more than 100 books for adults and children. She resides in northern New England with her husband and son. One of her favorite pastimes is visiting schools to talk to children about the writing process.